Pheasant Hunting For Kids

Hunting and Fishing Book for Kids

By

Isiah Maxwell

© Copyright 2018

All rights reserved.

The content contained within this book may not be reproduced, duplicated or transmitted without direct written permission from the author or the publisher.

Under no circumstances will any blame or legal responsibility be held against the publisher, or author, for any damages, reparation, or monetary loss due to the information contained within this book. Either directly or indirectly.

Legal Notice:

This book is copyright protected. This book is only for personal use. You cannot amend, distribute, sell, use, quote or paraphrase any part, or the content within this book, without the consent of the author or publisher.

Disclaimer Notice:

Please note the information contained within this document is for educational and entertainment purposes only. All effort has been executed to present accurate, up to date, and reliable, complete information. No warranties of any kind are declared or implied. Readers acknowledge that the author is not engaging in the rendering of legal, financial, medical or professional advice. The content within this book has been derived from various sources. Please consult a licensed professional before attempting any techniques outlined in this book.

By reading this document, the reader agrees that under no circumstances is the author responsible for any losses, direct or indirect, which are incurred as a result of the use of information contained within this document, including, but not limited to, — errors, omissions, or inaccuracies.

Pheasant Hunting for Kids

Table Of Contents

Introduction 6

Chapter 1: *Why Bagging Birds Is Fun* 9

Chapter 2: *Equipment to Bring* 14
    Hunting License 14
    A Map 15
    Shotgun 16
    Blaze Orange Clothes 17
    Glasses And Earmuffs 19
    Food 20
    Boots 21
    Dogs 22
    A First Aid Kit 23

Chapter 3: *Tips and Tricks* 25
    Be Quiet 25
    Be Patient 26
    Don't Hunt Large Expanses 27
    Get a Bird Dog 28
    Look For Water Sources 29
    Pheasant Signs 30
    Rainy or Snowy is Good 30

Chapter 4: *Safety Measures* 32

Chapter 5: *Animal Conservation* 36

Wildlife is Public Property 37

There Are Laws Protecting Wildlife 38

A Purpose for Wildlife Hunting 38

Chapter 6: *Glossary of Some Common Terms* .. *39*

Conclusion 41

Introduction

In a bid to get closer to nature and away from the hustle and rush of urban society, many have begun to introduce their kids to the fun and excitement of hunting pheasants. It's a great way for parents to bond with their wards in an environment that is both recreational and removed from the distractions of the Internet and other forms of media. Although, hunting has evolved from its compulsory past, it still has its uses in today's world.

In ancient times, humans had to hunt to survive each day. It was not a sport or anything of the like. Fast forward to modern times and life has progressed with such monumental strides that the need to stalk animals in the forest and kill them to sustain our lives has been cancelled out. Nowadays, people hunt for the purpose of achieving a sense of accomplishment, fostering stronger bonds and relaxing from the artificial life of the 21stcentury. In the process of hunting, most people find that they develop an immense appreciation for nature and the environment around them.

Hunting, although considered by so many to be a violent act, plays an invaluable role in nature. If done right, with respect for the animals being hunted, it allows for the smooth continuation of the cycle of life. It is an established fact that if all the predators in the wild were to stop hunting, the quick rise in the population of some animals may go beyond what is sustainable by our planet. Man, as we all know, has always been a member of this hunter category.

Some people stress the point that it was man's hunting which was responsible for the extinction of many animal species. Yet, this may not entirely be true. Besides the fact that some animals just weren't fit enough to continue surviving, one cannot blame hunting for the irresponsible and thoughtless actions of a number of people. Despite how fun something might be, there are limits to how far a person can go. Some folks go over the line in an attempt to satisfy the excitement started by hunting. Self-control and discipline is always the watchword, yet, nothing takes from the fact that hunting is beneficial to both man, animal and nature.

We will be exploring everything from how fun bagging a pheasant could be and why. We will also be looking at some tips and tricks to help you bag your first birdie and safety rules to ensure that you don't hurt yourself in the process.

I hope you enjoy reading this book and that it gives you a new outlook on pheasant hunting; one that appreciates nature, the beauty of pheasants and the limits of hunting.

Chapter 1

Why Bagging Birds Is Fun

Graceful, strong, big and colorful with a tail that seems to touch the very sky, the pheasant is indeed a beautiful and awe-inspiring bird. They are of a family of birds called Phasianidae and are diversified into about 49 species. This means there are so many of them in the world, that you could never get bored watching them go about their day. Just as man is believed to have originated in Africa, pheasants are said to have begun their lives in the continent of Asia. Unfortunately, careless hunting practices have made it so that very few pheasants are left in Asia anymore. This is why, before you even set out to hunt, you must understand that there is a limit to the things we should do. The opportunity to hunt any species of game must be appreciated as an honor. Use that time to observe certain things about the pheasant. Notice their similarities to chickens, and also make a note of the strong differences. Ask what some of their specialized parts have been adapted for. Do you see the claws hanging from their feet? How about their strong beaks? How quickly is a pheasant able to sense danger and how does it fight or run from this perceived danger?

Even though they share a few physiological attributes with chickens, pheasants are able to fly and sustain themselves in the air for much longer. Despite this, they prefer, like the chicken, to escape from trouble by running instead of flying. Their wings do not spread out like other flying bird but are rounded, again, like the chicken's. The male pheasants fight other males for dominance. Territories and females pheasants are some of the rewards of these fights. The males are usually the most colorful, as this is a great way to attract the females.

In a world that is becoming increasingly more taken with the indoor lifestyle, pheasant hunting is a safe and enjoyable way to enjoy the outdoors. Guided by their parents, young children can experience a stronger sense of accomplishment that can be gotten from a video game. They learn to set goals and appreciate life to its fullest. Many parents who used to struggle with getting through to their kids or holding their attention for any duration of time, have found hunting to be a great way to relate with them. Hunting is one activity that cuts through every generation and can't be said to be old-fashioned. The laughter and pride shared between parent and child after a bird has been bagged is pure and authentic.

Aided by a guide (this could be the parent or a professional) and hunting dogs, kids can set out confidently for a memorable wildlife experience. They learn the art of patiently waiting for the right moment and the elation of making a kill. They also learn, in the process, how to handle a gun; a lesson which could come in handy for any child. They are taught the correct posture for pointing a gun, how to take aim and when to shoot. They also learn how to track down the bird and take home the prize.

Regardless of how violent an image this may play

in the minds of parents and kids alike, it is not nearly as bad as that. Kids should not be deprived of this fun and freeing experience. Kids in the past did not turn evil from hunting but, instead, grew up with observational skills and a keen appreciation for nature.

Hunting in the wild teaches kids to be tough, resilient and equips them with the ability to make do with smallest and most basic resources; lessons which are invaluable in any time and society. Setting a goal and seeing that it is fulfilled is another skill which guarantees success even outside the hunting arena. Being able to hold one's ground and be steady in the face of daunting odds are added life lessons which a child could benefit immensely from.

While hunting, normally reclusive children have been known to become more outspoken and audacious, throwing banters and laughing happily. Kids are challenged in the wild to give their best while having fun at it. Hunting is not at all what it has been painted to be. Children should be allowed to partake in the life-enriching experience as they grow to become more productive and observant.

Chapter 2

Equipment to Bring

In addition to the sheer joy of the pheasant hunting experience, a few things could make it so that it is not nearly as difficult as it could be. They allow for a seamless fun time in the wild. Below are a few of the necessary equipment.

Hunting License

You may believe that rules are made only to be broken in the end, but this not the case with pheasant hunting. These regulations are given to protect both humans and wildlife. Breaking them attracts very severe penalties. Very few hunters go into the wild with the intention of breaking a laid down law but, as is said, ignorance is no excuse. Unaware that an action is unacceptable by law, many hunters behave carelessly and land themselves in avoidable hot water. One of these rules is that a hunter must be licensed before he or she can go into the wild to hunt game. They must also carry their license with them at all times to prove the legality of their activities in the wild. Hunters are also advised to carry a hunting regulation with them. This will guide and prevent them from making an ignorant mistake, which would then attract legal action against them. There are hunting time periods, as well as a limit to how much game, in this case, pheasants, a hunter can bag. There are areas in the wild that are prohibited from hunters; a regulation would inform you about this and save you from trouble.

A Map

Hunters can be considered to be adventurers of sorts, and what is an adventure without a trusty map. The best hunting locations can be revealed with an educated look at a map, and they are not so difficult to obtain too. A simple visit to a wildlife agency or their website is enough. Also, despite what has been previously said about the 21st century in this book, they did provide resources like Google maps. This has turned out be almost every hunter's surest guide. Google maps can be zoomed in to give a more accurate picture of prohibited and prime locations.

Shotgun

This is one of the most important aspects of pheasant hunting. Choosing the right gun for the right hunter is a decision that should not be taken lightly. More experienced hunters may be more comfortable using a 12 gauge shotgun, but the novices should be encouraged to wield the same. A 20 gauge shotgun would be more fitting for a child. At most, parents may get a 16 gauge shotgun for their kids to use in hunting pheasants. What is important is that the kids should be taught how to comfortably fire one. When you visit the gun shop, ask to see an autoloader, a Browning Citori, a Steger and an over-and-under. They have different capabilities and the trick would be finding which is the best fit for your child. Your choice should be one that isn't too heavy to handle and that reloads quickly enough. Still, you shouldn't have to break the bank to afford a shotgun. Ask other customers at the shop or the shopkeeper or do a Google search to determine the appropriate gun for your child's age. The Browning Citori is usually the more expensive one, while the autoloader is quite heavy.

Guns should be handled carefully and with the proper posture. There have been confirmed reports in the past of people becoming casualties of self-inflicted gunshot injuries as a result of poor gun handling. With the proper knowledge, your kid will be safe while he has an adventure hunting pheasants.

Blaze Orange Clothes

Unfortunately, some hunters have been known to defy this rule and things didn't turn out well in the end. In some places, it is more than a mere suggestion that a hunter should wear, above his waist, at least a piece of clothing in blaze orange. This is a sharp color and it is almost impossible to miss. Whilst in the jungle or in other hunting locations, hunting parties may be so far apart from each other that it may be extremely difficult to tell a human from an animal, especially when the animal or human passes suddenly in the distance. This blaze orange is recommended and sometimes required to be worn by hunters before they take on the wild.

Since the head of a hunter is usually the first to be seen, especially when they are in a low position such as down a hill, it is a good safety practice to wear blaze orange caps. This is depicted well in cartoons, where young troopers or hunters are shown in the wild with blaze orange clothing. There is no point putting yourself needlessly in harm's way.

Some days in the wild will be warm, hot or cold. If you must go hunting on a day with less than favorable weather conditions or temperature, then dress to match those conditions. Depending on how cold the temperature is, you may wear a parka or a jacket. On hot days, the less clothing you wear the better, and it goes without saying, that red carpet fashion would be improper for hunting activities. The danger senses of a pheasant are very alert and their four-toed feet, very fast. Hunting one would require you to dress in clothes that allows you to get as close to the ground as possible. They should also be free enough for you to move quickly in them. You will find pheasants in less than pretty habitats. You should be dressed appropriately for these places. Whatever type of clothing you decide to purchase for your hunting expedition, it should be one that will protect your skin from thorny branches and the likes.

Glasses And Earmuffs

Even though your kids have been taught how to properly shoot a gun, protective glasses are still a necessary component of hunting gears. An unfortunate lapse in judgment or a malfunction could mean serious eye problems. Also, some paths in the woods are thick with berry bushes, others with thorns hanging out, which could get in a person's eye and cause severe damage. The sun is another factor of concern when hunting pheasants. Aiming at one that has taken to the air without protective glasses, could have the harsh glare of the sun focused in your eyes. When purchasing these glasses, select those that are colored. If it is yellow, then all the better.

An earmuff is a very important protective gear for children. When a shot is fired, the sound may be too much for their young ears. Also, they are usually the cheapest of all hunting equipment to purchase, with some going for as little as a dollar or less. As such, there isn't much of a reason why earmuffs should not be bought for children as part of their protective hunting gear.

Food

Pheasant hunting is rough and busy, with very little time to sit in one spot for too long a time. It is far removed from the sedentary lifestyle of normal city life. Because of this, you may need to constantly refuel from time to time. Energy spent chasing down pheasants should be renewed to avoid dizziness and fainting spells. More important than any snack you may decide to carry along with you is water. Water is considered to be the most precious commodity for hunters in the wild. This is more true when the temperature is significantly high. Dehydration occurs quickly and could lead to sluggishness. Sports drinks are a good way to refuel your body after it has lost a substantial amount of electrolytes. Fruits are also essential in the wild. In fact, they are the best snack to have with you as you have fun hunting.

Boots

Again, pheasants are very quick on their feet and hunting them will lead you to some harsh habitats. This challenging situation can be overcome to a point. You need to wear the right boots. If you're going to be a hunter, you can't be walking about in the wild dressed in shoes fit for offices or runways. Ankle-high boots are a good way to go in dressing up for pheasant hunting. If you can though, purchase boots that go above your ankle. Pheasants are sometimes found in marshlands and other places with water. It is an unpleasant feeling to move about for hours in wet or soggy boots. Purchase the right kind of boots for a fun pheasant hunting experience.

Dogs

Retrievers and spaniels and other species of hunting dogs are truly man's best friend whilst out in the wild. Their keen sense of smell, hearing and instinctive behavior makes it easy for them to locate prey, whether dead or alive. They should be well-trained and healthy in order to be effective in sensing prey. When bringing water and fruit for yourself while hunting, don't forget to also bring for your dog. They get tired too and their strength needs to be replenished. If you do not treat them in this way, it may not be reasonable to expect so much from them.

A dog can only do the things it has learned. If you do not train it to hunt, you may spend an entire day urging it to no end. Yelling at them will not yield the desired results and it is pointless and wrong to beat a dog. Train them and make sure they are healthy and fit to spend any amount of time hunting with you. If you do this, you will find dogs to be the best companions for a productive and fun hunting day.

A First Aid Kit

To be outdoors in the wild hunting an animal as flighty as a pheasant without a fully stocked first aid kit, is unimaginable. Pheasant hunting involves a lot of activities, and injuries are very likely to occur sometimes. From falling over while running, to getting scratched by thorns or leaves, a first aid kit must be available to prevent minor injuries from becoming infected. No hunting gear is complete without a first aid kit and there should be someone present who knows how to use its contents.

Chapter 3

Tips and Tricks

There is a method to getting the best results out of anything. Whether it's reading for a test, playing soccer or hunting pheasants, you need an understanding of how to be productive in that activity. Below are a few tips to guide your hunting experience and ensure you have the best time in the wild:

Be Quiet

You know how soldiers in movies walk stealthily, using hand signals to communicate with each other, in order to avoid alerting criminals of your presence? You would have to behave in much the same way when you go pheasant hunting. Although the stakes may not be as high as in soldiers trying to capture a terrorist gang, pheasants are very attentive to their surroundings.

This is especially true for those amongst them who have been hunted, but survived, in time past. Heavy footsteps, the slam of a car door and loud conversations are enough to send these birds looking for shelter or running far away from danger so, if you are going to hunt a pheasant, do it stealthily. Find your inner soldier.

Be Patient

You're not going to get anything done by hurrying and chasing the wind. You need to be patient and observe the feeding patterns of these birds. Most pheasants prefer to come out of hiding during evening time. At this time, there is less light and they can move through grassy terrains without being discovered by already-tired hunters. This is not to say that it is impossible to hunt pheasants during any other time of the day, but you may have to be patient to get the best hunting done. When out the wild, keep your voice and other activities quiet, and observe the possible hideouts of pheasants. When one is located, do not rush in to catch them. Also, do not, in a fit of excitement, start shooting from very long distances. Behave in the same way as predators do. Stalk them and wait for the precise moment – the moment when the range is close enough for your shot to have a better chance of hitting home. When the time is just right - strike.

Don't Hunt Large Expanses

Doing so is a good way to go about wasting an entire day with nothing to show for it. It is not advisable to hunt every square meter of a particular habitat. After all, pheasants do not often walk in the open. You are more like to catch a pheasant if you hunt around the perimeters of a habitat. Basically, if you would hunt in places that are closer to the edges, or the edges themselves, you will find your ringnecks. Be calculated when it has to do with pheasant hunting. Do not move into an area hinting ignorantly and hoping for the best. Pheasant hunting, as has been stated earlier, is a bit rough but definitely an energy-sapping activity.

It becomes quite disappointing when you have to return home without a single catch. Do your research, consult the Internet, ask fellow hunters and read a map to locate the best places where pheasants are most likely to be. This will cut down your hunting time and produce a more satisfying result.

Get a Bird Dog

To locate pheasants in thick grass, cattails and other hiding spots would require the sharpened senses of a trained bird dog. These dogs possess the uncanny ability to sniff out pheasants from all manner of hiding places and guide the hunter to them. Sometimes, after flushing the bird and taking it down, the problem becomes a matter of finding the downed birds. Bird dogs are excellent for these tasks. Without a bird dog by your side, you may spend a full day toiling different habitats, taking down a few birds and going home with nothing. These bird dogs, which could be spaniel or labs, will save you from walking fruitlessly looking for dead or live birds.

Look For Water Sources

During the dry weather, pheasants will move out to look for water in order to stay hydrated. In this season, it's more productive to hunt closer to watering holes, rivers, irrigation canals and the likes. This is one behavior that is typical of every warm-blooded animal and has been confirmed by experienced hunters and scientists alike. Do not make the error of thinking that the pheasants will leave themselves completely exposed, as to be easily shot at by hunters, as they will still be in cover, even in these locations, and their senses will still be very alert. One quick and heavy footstep and your rooster will take off. You are very like to bag many birds closer to water sources in hot weathers, but you would still be required to behave like a hunter, so as not to set the pheasants off.

Pheasant Signs

How can you tell that an area is likely to be populated by pheasants? If you can't, then your hunting experience may be a difficult one. There are several signs which betray the existence of pheasants in a particular location. The most obvious for anyone is when they are seen crossing the road as hunters make their way to hunting fields. Another obvious pointer is the crowing of these birds, especially in the mornings, but a less experienced hunter may not know that pheasants gravitate towards cattails. The thicker the cattail, the better it is for a hunter to hide. Since corn is a good part of their diet, it is also a telltale that pheasants just might be somewhere around that habitat.

Rainy or Snowy is Good

Newbie hunters may find it a little difficult to comprehend, but it is generally agreed by experienced hunters that pheasants are easier to bag during the rainy or snowy seasons. Bird dogs have a better chance of sniffing out the hiding spots of live pheasants or places where the downed birds are. It could also be much more fun for you if you let it be. Think about it. Walking in your waterproof boots and hunting with the cool air breezing about. The rainy season is the best for both bird dogs and hunters. Snow, on the other hand, is good because you can track down the pheasants from their distinctive footsteps.

Chapter 4

Safety Measures

Flaunting safety rules may not only prove harmful to you, but to the other hunters sharing the same expanse of land as you. This is why you must ensure that you're not only healthy enough to go hunting, but that all your hunting equipment is in top shape. Follow the safety measures below and you'll always return from a hunting trip well and happy:

- Get enough sleep before setting out in the morning. Do not spend the entire night watching TV, clicking away on your phone or playing video games. Feeling tired early into a hunt, or falling asleep in a field, could prove to be hazardous. Also, you are not likely to bag a pheasant when your mind is aimed at sleep.

- Make certain, at all times, that the safety of

your gun is always on. If you are not ready to shoot at a bird, do not disengage your gun's safety. This is to avoid an unfortunate case of accidental shooting. Also, make sure it is clean, even before leaving the house. A well-maintained gun is less likely to jam or misfire.

- Do not forget your blaze orange. Whether you choose to wear an orange cap or vest, make sure it is on. It could, literally, mean the difference between life and death. Help fellow hunters to easily locate you by standing out with your distinctive blaze orange.

- Make sure your finger is well away from the gun's trigger. Unless you are aiming at a pheasant, the muzzle of the gun should not be pointed at anyone or anything, and your finger must not be placed on the trigger. If the bird is not flying, then you must be careful in ensuring that no person or animal is behind the pheasant. Also, do not fire at hard surfaces, to avoid the bullet ricocheting and hitting you, the bird dog or a fellow hunter.

- Try not to walk in front of another hunter. Mistakes have happened with inexperienced shooters accidentally firing at another person. Walk shoulder to shoulder if you can.

- It is expected that a child would behave like a child every time. This means that they would be playful and forgetful at times. It is irresponsible to leave to hunt without the supervision of an adult. Children should also be taught safety rules and the dangers of flaunting them. It can truly be fun and games if these safety measures are kept by parents and children alike.

- Do not leave home without a well-charged phone. There is always the possibility of an emergency occurring while hunting, and remember to carry a compass with you. It could be frustrating or scary even, to get lost while hunting pheasants. With a compass and a fully charged smartphone, these eventualities can be avoided.

When you have decided to go hunting, make it like a mission. Research on the habitat you have chosen to know its unique features and history. Clean your gun in the proper manner and oil the parts that demand it. Check that your first aid kit is fully stocked, wear your hunting appropriate clothes, pack your phone, food, water, compass and other necessary hunting equipment and, finally, get a license to hunt in that area.

Chapter 5

Animal Conservation

To conserve a thing is to prevent it from being used up completely. When it refers to animals, it is a way of protecting the biodiversity in nature and prevent certain species of animals from going extinct. It may be permissible by law to hunt particular animals, but there are limits which must not be trespassed. Where the hunting of an animal begins to dangerously affect the survival of its species, is where the line must be drawn and all hunting activities on that animal called off.

Hunting, by itself, could be employed as a means to conserving an animal (pheasants, in this case) and ensuring the continuation of its species if it is done right. It all depends on the history of that animal, the laws of the land and other important factors. Zimbabwe is one country where this proves true. By controlling the population growth of some animals with responsible hunting practices, they have ensured that these animals will continue to survive for longer than they would have. Yet, countries like Kenya have banned hunting practices to some degree, because of the dangerous toll it was taking on wildlife.

Consider the points below to help you get a better grasp of animal conservation:

Wildlife is Public Property

Unless an animal is domesticated, it cannot be said to belong to you. This means that if you were to capture an animal in the wild, you could be questioned and sanctioned for doing so. An area of land may belong to you, but the wildlife on it is public property. Permission must be granted to you by the relevant authorities to either hunt or capture them.

Do Not Sell Native Animals This is not so much a suggestion as it is a law. There is no legal market to accommodate the transaction of wild deer meat, eagle feathers and so on. Although licensed hunters may be granted permission to hunt, if an animal is native to a particular place, none of its parts may be sold.

There Are Laws Protecting Wildlife

The Endangered Species Protection Act and The Marine Mammal Protection Act are but a few laws which prevent certain species of animals from being hunted into extinction. Even with a license, these animals must not be hunted and individuals have to be careful to not break these government laws.

A Purpose for Wildlife Hunting

Trophy hunting is one activity that must be shunned against. It is demeaning of animal kind and has entirely no reasonable purpose to it. Wildlife conservation activities makes it so that there are limits to how many birds can be bagged in a single hunting expedition and what the meat can be used for.

Chapter 6

Glossary of Some Common Terms

Covey - These refer to a group of pheasants who flush or roost together.

Cover - Bushes, grass and other types of vegetation which serve as a hiding place for pheasants. They stay in these places to avoid been seen by hunters or other predators.

Flush - This is what hunters do when they chase pheasants from their cover. Most often, these pheasants fly from their cover and make it easy for hunters to take aim and shoot at them.

Gauge - This is the size of the bore of a shotgun, the diameter precisely. The smaller it is, the better. Experienced hunters prefer 12-gauge shotguns to the less powerful 20-gauge shotguns.

Bag - To shoot at and kill a pheasant. There is a

daily limit to how many pheasants can be bagged by a single hunter.

Clay pigeon - Hunters use this to practice their aim. They try to simulate a bird in flight by throwing a disc made of clay into the air and shooting it.

Over-and-under - This is a type of double-barreled shotgun. It allows the hunter to make two shots successively.

Roosting - This is a type of hunting where individuals try to locate the resting spots of pheasants at night.

Conclusion

Pheasant hunting is a fun activity to be enjoyed by the whole family. The life lessons and opportunities to create an even deeper bond between parents and their children is one that should not be missed but, even as fun and as recreational as pheasant hunting might be, the safety measures involved should not be overlooked. Kids should be taught how to handle shotguns properly, and their limits, while out hunting game. They should also be taught to treat their dogs with respect. Kids are likely to become impatient and start screaming at their dogs. They must understand that this is wrong and that patience is rewarding.

Printed in Great Britain
by Amazon